BEYOND THE WALLS

FREEDOM IS CALLING

Rosalind S. Elliott

Copyright © 2017 Rosalind S. Elliott

All rights reserved. No portion of this book may be reproduced, stored in a retrieval system, or transmitted in any form or by any means-----electronic mechanical, photocopy, recording, scanning or other—except for brief quotations in reviews or articles, without the express prior written permission of the publisher.

Unless otherwise noted, all scripture quotations are taken from the New International Version of the Bible (Public Domain www.biblegateway.com). Other scripture references are from

ISBN-13: 978-0-6929-7900-6

Printed in the United States of America.

DEDICATION

I would like to dedicate this book to everyone who has ever felt lost and broken. To the challenges that almost broke me, I give you a huge smile because you didn't win!

To the apple of my eye, Kenneth, and my son Landon. To my parents, Wallace and Betty. To my brother, Adrian. To Mama Lee, Kim, Daniel. Each of you have inspired me, encouraged me, and embraced me in your own way. Thank you for loving me.

To my true friends, I won't name each of you but you know who you are. Your prayers, your realness, and your compassion are invaluable to me. I couldn't have survived without you.

To my pastor and my church family Rock Hill Baptist, thank you for your prayers and love. Thank you all for being in my life.

CONTENTS

	Introduction	viii
1	Trapped	1
2	Hush	13
3	In the Dark	23
4	See the Light	33
5	Get Up and Fight	43
6	Go For It	56
7	Distractions	63
8	Sound the Trumpet	72
	Note from the Author	79
	Daily Affirmations	82
	Reflections	83
	Acknowledgements	84
	Resources	86
	About the Author	88

INTRODUCTION

The walls of a house are separated into two categories: loadbearing or non-loadbearing. Loadbearing walls support their own weight and the weight of other parts of the house. The roof and the floors. Non-loadbearing walls carry their own weight. They are independent of other structural components of a house. If you decide to do renovations or additional construction to your house, it's important that you know the difference so that you won't destroy your house.

Similarly, like construction workers we put up walls too. Our walls are the residue of bad experiences trapped within our minds. The loadbearing walls are built from an offense. The non-loadbearing walls are constructed as the result of an offense. We easily turn what is nothing into pure chaos when we let our minds be idle. Aren't you tired of being offended and bound? It's time to free yourself. Forgiveness is waiting. Love is patiently awaiting you to let it in again. Let the real "you" stand up!

I understand that you may be enduring one of the hardest seasons of your life. You're not alone. I've been there too but I came out. And here I am now, talking to you telling you that you can escape from your walls too.

When I decided to write this book, it wasn't during the easiest time of my life, that's for sure. I was torn between accepting my calling into ministry and walking away from everything. I wasn't even sure if I really should write this book. My mind was not quite open yet to sharing my journey with you. But as always, God has the final say so it became a part of my assignment. That's the whole purpose of me writing to you. It's part of my purpose. I was put on this earth to encourage and uplift others. Is it a piece of cake to do this? Of course not! But I must do my part to make a change in the world but to also make a change within me.

While writing this book, I found out that there were still things that I had not reconciled.

I still had some dark spots around my heart that needed checking out. I had to confront me.

Now, I'm asking you to do the same. Confront you. Find your own dark spots in the nooks and crannies of your heart chambers. Delve into the deep secrets, the shame, and the guilt and even into the hatred. It will be painful, ugly, and uncomfortable. But it will be worth it.

Everything that you have ever gone through in life was for this moment. Why? Well, you found this book—maybe through no fault of your own but thankfully, you're still reading. We have a journey to take together. When it gets hard, always remember that you are never on this journey alone. I will be checking in on you just as if we were side by side. I want you to not only live but thrive.

Let's take our masks off and enjoy the ride. It's time to go beyond the walls. I believe that at the end of our journey, God will give beauty for ashes.

THE WALL

Obstacles don't have to stop you. If you run into a wall, don't turn around and give up. Figure out how to climb it, go through it, or work around it.

- Michael Jordan

1

TRAPPED

Moreover, no one knows when their hour will come: As fish are caught in a snare, so people are trapped by evil times that fall unexpectedly upon them. -Ecclesiastes 9:12

The phone rang. It's too early to get a phone call. It's my daddy. Why is he calling me so early? I was not prepared for what I was about to hear. "Your grandma passed away this morning around…are you okay?" That phone called played over and over and over in my head. Surely, this wasn't happening for real. The woman who helped raise me. Who always listened to me. You mean to tell me she's gone? Dead!

When reality sunk in, I lost it. Deep down inside, I knew it was coming. I just didn't think it would be so soon. That day I felt like my life had been turned completely upside down. Her death to me seemed to be the catalyst to start the time clock for death within our family. I simply was not ready. But you never are. Nothing can prepare you for death.

So, what do you do when your life as you know it falls apart suddenly? In my case, I became a functional depressant. I was happy in public and depressed at home.

During this particular time when my grandma passed away, nothing seemed to work well for me and I was tired. I was angry at God. Why did He allow this to happen? Why didn't He heal her? Why couldn't I say goodbye to her first?

Then I felt regret. I should have said yes to bring her to the wedding. I could have at least had that moment to cherish. Thought after thought of would have, could have, and should have uprooted me so much that I turned my back on my relationship with God. I would go to church just because it was routine. I didn't want anyone to suspect something was wrong. Those were some bad times. Have you been there before? Are you there now?

There are some circumstances or situations that happen in life that we are not supposed to deal with alone. We were never supposed to carry burdens alone. When you do, you start putting up walls in places you didn't know were available for a wall.

Truthfully speaking, I was offended by what God had allowed. That one offense turned into me being defensive. I shut my family and friends out and I figured the less I engaged with them, the less hurt I would be if something happened to one of them. I put up a loadbearing wall so high that you would think I was building a skyscraper.

My walls were the three things that I wrestled with: grief, identity theft, and offense.

Research and studies show that there are five stages to grief. Denial. Anger. Bargaining.

Depression and Acceptance. Some people skip stages and some experience all stages.

The one area that is the most dangerous if you never reach it is "Acceptance". Acceptance only comes after you've realized that the situation isn't going to change and you change your perspective of the traumatic circumstance. It doesn't mean that you don't have periodic bursts of denial, anger, bargaining, or depression. It simply means that you have developed a way to cope that won't destroy your mental state. Staying in any of the other stages too long can be detrimental to your emotional well-being.

For me, I couldn't stay in denial because the very thing I wanted to deny stared me in the face the day of the funeral. But anger and depression? I wallowed in it. Trust me when I say it was not the best time of my life. I lost who I was and I had no idea who I was becoming. When you lose sight of who you are, your self-esteem and confidence will plummet and the simplest things irritate you beyond measure.

I wasn't happy. I was miserable. I didn't have a life. I would come home from work, do my wifely duties, and go to bed. That's not the way anyone's life should be. We've been given life to enjoy. Sure, life happens but we should never let life dictate our enjoyment and appreciation for being here. I put up walls in almost every area of my life, both loadbearing and non-loadbearing walls.

What loadbearing or non-loadbearing walls are you carrying? And do you know the difference?

If you don't know, check your foundation. Your foundation is your belief system and the types of thoughts that you allow to infiltrate your mind. A house without a solid foundation will eventually fall, leaving you trapped inside.

Something interesting that I learned about Canada is that they have three main traps that they use to catch animals: the leg-hold trap, the conibear trap, and the snare trap. Each trap has its own level of cruelty.

The leg-hold trap is designed to capture an

animal just passing through. The animal becomes immobile and after time is unable to fight off potential danger. The leg-hold trap weakens the animal's natural fight so much that it begins to do anything and everything to get free. Even biting or chewing its own flesh to break free. Often, the animal dies of blood loss or is wounded so severely that its quality of life is poor which shortens the animal's life expectancy.

The conibear trap is a two-part trap that lets the animal suffer longer by clamping shut on the body of the animal. The animal is left defenseless. What's unique about this particular trap is that the conditions have to be right. The animal has to be the right size, traveling at the right speed, entering in the trap at the right angle.

The last and final trap, the snare is a tricky one. Its most often used to catch foxes and bears and it is not easily seen. In fact, in some places it can even be placed in trees. Animals caught in a snare are usually strangled to death.

Now, let's take these same traps and apply them to mental traps.

The leg-hold trap represents those things that we don't realize have a hold on us until it's too late and the pain of it manifests in public ways. It can also spread over into the lives of our loved ones. Much like the animal, we become immobile.

The conibear trap causes excruciating pain unlike the other traps because it's two-fold. The devastation from the blow of it can leave you incapacitated, cutting off your circulation of hope. As your hope begins to diminish, the infection of desperation starts to spread. This trap rattles you deeply because it challenges everything you know and believe.

Last but certainly not least is the snare. While it might not seem like the most dangerous, it is the most unpredictable. Snares can be really sneaky. Some snares have food that tempt the prey into an action. They are easily disguised and there is always an element of deception. The surprise of the snare is never in the design but in the craftiness used to trap. There are three things that concern me about a snare. You don't know where it is. You don't know who set it. And you don't know how long the pain of it will last.

Isn't it ironic how these physical traps can be explained as mental traps? Well, a trap is a trap and it doesn't care who it catches.

I don't know about you but tight spaces make me cringe and panic. I get an overwhelming feeling of anxiety with an urge to get out. A term for this response is called acute stress response better known as fight or flight response. It is a physiological reaction based on a perceived thought of harm or attack. But one of the things that I've learned is that when you're trapped, your natural defense mechanisms don't function properly. Why? Because your foundation has cracks and you've inserted walls where there should be open spaces.

It's not normal to be closed off and withdrawn. Even God wanted communion and relationship because He created Adam and Eve.

See, many of our problems wouldn't be magnified in our minds so much if we just told someone we needed help or we needed to talk. Let's face it. Trying to navigate life alone is burdensome. Nobody should have to do it yet there are people who do. Unfortunately, because of this, there are over 25 million Americans who suffer with some form of depression.

Shocking?

It should be. But it's reality. Just let that sink in.

Are you one of the 25 million Americans? If you are, do something about it before it does something about you. The grip of depression and anxiety is real. You can't overcome it if you keep silent. You also can't heal what you refuse to confront. Confession is good for the soul and the truth sets you free. If you're trapped, it's okay. You just have to deal with those things that have you trapped.

Understand that the first step in any program of recovery is admitting you have a problem. With addicts, the problem is never the alcohol or the drugs. It's what led them to the alcohol or the drugs. The alcohol or the drugs were just byproducts of the actual problem. Likewise, being trapped is not the problem. It's how you fell into the trap. The health issues, the anger and resentment, and the substance abuse are just byproducts. To get to the root of any problem, you have to go back to the source. My source was God. I needed to find my way back to Him but I could only do it if I allowed myself to get back to Him. I had to give myself permission to be led in the dark to get to the light.

See traps aren't designed to free you. They are designed to keep you secured in position to immobilize you. The longer you're trapped the more self-destructive you become.

Even in my darkest hours of being trapped, I was never alone. Yes, it felt like I was, but I wasn't. And you are not alone either. Let me say it again. You are not alone. In my times of distress, I began to write just to get out my feelings. These writings are actually some of what you are reading. If you don't feel comfortable at first talking with someone, try journaling like I did.

There is always a way out of every situation. It may take you seeking outside assistance but by all means, don't stay where you are. Talk with a friend or a confidante. But take ownership of who you are and where you are at this particular moment in your life. Talk to somebody. In my case, I needed to talk to God.

Let me share with you a letter that I wrote about me. In the letter, I imagined what God would have said to me at my low moment.

After you read it, take a moment and think about what yours might say.

Dear Rosalind,

What are you afraid of? Are you really concerned about what people will think or are you more concerned about what their thoughts will confirm? You can't hold yourself hostage to please anyone else. You missed opportunities. Not because they weren't available but because you failed to walk through the doors I held open for you. It stared you in the face and when you thought you could run from it, it taunted you. Unrealized dreams. They turned into your nightmares. Unrealized hope. You began to slip into an abyss. You were in a deep hole that you refused to see there was an opening. All you had to do was want to escape. Take back your rightful place in your dreams. Replace your battered hope with renewed faith and only then will you realize who you are. You can be free to be who I called you to be. Come here my child. I'm waiting for you. I'm standing at the altar of your heart waiting for you to let me in again. Because you are my greatest creation.

With Love,

Abba, the Father

2

HUSH

Silence can be deafening.

Growing up in the south, when someone says "Hush!" you hush. The finality in the tone of the word makes you not question anything. You just keep your mouth closed and you don't open it until you've been asked a question directly. For many of us, "hushing" is all we know but sometimes hushing shuts us down permanently.

I've been a church girl nearly all of my life. Because of this, I know that many people who attend church are hiding something. On any given Sunday, you'll see gorgeous suits and ties, beautiful flowing dresses and hats, designer bags and shoes. Then, that is where the imagery stops. On the surface, we all look great! Underneath the surface, it's not always so pleasant.

There are secrets. Hidden agendas. Broken dreams. Failures and disappointments. All because something or someone told us to hush.

Since I've alluded to church, let's keep going with this setting so I can illustrate how this works. In this illustration, the you are the character. Just take a deep breath and become the character.

You get out of the car and you walk slowly to the doors of the church. You are greeted with warm welcomes and handshakes. When you get to the doors, your thoughts are confused. It's the first time you've been to church in years. You think to yourself, should I open the door or leave?

You found the courage to open the door because you need encouragement and an encounter with God to help lift the sadness and despair off of you. Thoughts about how much you cried the night before into the morning kept replaying in your mind. You only fell asleep last night because you had no tears left. Nobody can feel the weight of the pressure that holds your heart down except you. As you turn the knob, the door of the church creaks open. An usher greets you and motions for you to have a seat. You sit. Your palms are sweaty so you start glancing over the order of service. This time you are ready to hear the speaker.

Then, it happened. Some powerful voice sings the words, "Pass me not O gentle Savior, hear my humble cry..." The tears you held back seemed to burst forward as the song continued. *Something within you is breaking free.* As your heart beats faster, the speaker gives a stirring message that continues to tug at your heart. You've made up in your mind that this time will be different. As you anxiously sit and wait in expectancy, your mind is racing but somehow you feel peace.

Out of nowhere, one of your thoughts says to you, "Now is your time!" until it rang so loud in your mind that everything seemed to stop. Words began to form with your mouth. They slowly changed to an audible whisper.

"Help! God help me! I need you!"

The speaker says, "If there is anyone who desires prayer. Let him come now to the altar.

When you finally get up the nerve to stand up, you look around. The choir is singing.

This is the perfect time.

As you make your way to the aisle, your eyes shift to the altar, then to the speaker. Then you look around one last time throughout the congregation. As you look at the faces of the people, fear and doubt kick in. You start questioning yourself.

How can I give my life to someone I can't see? Once they find out my past, there's no way they will accept me. Hold on, nobody's up there at the altar. I'm not about to be the only one up there.

Suddenly the peaceful voice that was compelling you to come, grew quiet, until there was silence. Without hesitation, you made your way back to your seat.

Being in situations such as this don't stop

with church. I simply used church as an example because I'm so familiar with it. Situations like this can happen anywhere. What you just witnessed was doubt trampling hope. For doubt is a powerful mechanism that can cripple any positive advance towards freedom - whether it's spiritual, physical, or emotional. Doubt is so powerful that it births fear.

Let me provide you with another example.

Suppose a friend asks you to go zip lining with them in the mountains and you decide to go. You think to yourself, it can't be that bad, right? So you hike up to the zip line area. As you listen to the safety instructor give the spill about safety, you drift off into space. You hear the instructor but you're really just going through the motions. After, you get harnessed in with the safety belts for a brief moment, you look down and start thinking. If your harness belt unbuckles or breaks, you will probably fall to an immediate death. Surveying the area, you see how far you have to zip-line to get to the other side. Instantly, you begin to doubt whether you can make it safely and fear takes over.

See how the seed of doubt created the fear. Once fear has manifested, it is an upward battle to overcome it and more often than not, we succumb to it. Fear takes what we know about ourselves and causes us to hush. We hush up our dreams. We hush up our aspirations. We do this so much until it silently kills our purposed identity.

The Discovery of the Hush Spirit

Now---there's not an actual definition or literal meaning of the "hush spirit" but I called it that because of what it does. A spirit is the nonphysical part of a person that is the seat of emotions and character but it is not to be confused with the soul. The full definition of hush is to calm, quiet, put at rest, or to keep from public knowledge. When you combine the two, you have a combination of psychological signals that trigger emotions to put your thoughts to rest or away from public knowledge. This happens to a lot of us.

As a young child, I had dreams of singing on the big stage in front of thousands of people. I would try to imitate the late great Whitney Houston's voice in front of a full-length mirror in my parents' bedroom when no one was around. When I was done with that, I would practice in the mirror like I was TLC trying to get their moves down. I know you might be laughing but don't judge me.

Through all of my fake performances, never once did it occur to me that I couldn't do it. I set the goal that I would make it big as a singer by 23 years old.

Time passed. I did a few talent shows during this time but I never won first place. It was always either an honorable mention or second place so I began to believe I wasn't good enough. To this day, I still don't think I'm where I need to be with singing.

People would tell me I had something but my belief in myself started to diminish. After a while, I started wondering if people were just being nice. Have you ever felt like that? At one point, I got so overwhelmed with comparison that my insecurities took over and I literally stopped singing for a while. Why did my insecurities take over you ask?

Well, the first thing I did wrong was try to compare myself to others. I didn't understand back then that everybody is called to a unique talent or skill that fits within a divine purpose. Another reason my insecurities bothered me so much was because I learned in a particular situation that the pigment of my skin chose my fate before I had a chance to demonstrate my skill.

During your formative teenage years, facing discrimination is a bitter pill to swallow. I simply wanted to do what I always wanted to do. The closer that I got to 23, the less enthusiastic I was about my singing career. To be quite honest, I didn't have one at all so by the time I graduated college at 22, those dreams and aspirations that I once had were hushed.

As time went on, I learned that nothing was wrong with my voice or me. It was my motives. All I wanted were tangible things. The glamorous life I saw on TV with the money, the houses, and the cars. But none of those things could give me the inner peace that I desired. I was trying to be someone who didn't align with my true self. The effects of it left me with walls of doubt, fear, and a whole host of insecurities and self-esteem battles.

We have to get to a point where we see beyond the physical things and see the big picture. If we don't, the "hush" will ring indefinitely in our ears. I can assure you that it is a noise that you can't drown out until you put things back into proper perspective.

Throughout my life, I've learned this the hard way. I let the silence overshadow my purpose until one day I got up the nerve to fight back against the trap. I was never destined to live a mediocre life and you weren't either.

Don't hide under what people see or say. Stand boldly on what you know to be true about yourself. Looking for approval in all the wrong places of your life will cast a shadow over each area of your life. You will constantly look for satisfaction from dry places. Come out from among the shadows. It's time to deal with what you have been refusing to confront. You can't heal what you won't discover. Now is the time for your personal altar call. Don't let your trap keep you from living your best life.

3

IN THE DARK

He reveals the deep things of darkness and brings utter darkness into the light. –Job 12:22

Recently, in South Carolina there was a total solar eclipse. Total solar eclipses occur when the moon comes between the sun and earth, to cast a full shadow of darkness on the earth. Millions of people came from all over the world to witness this miraculous event. I chose to stay inside and watch the environment. As the moon became closer to the sun, the sky darkened and the animals began to quiet. You could only hear the nocturnal animals. When it finally got to totality, there was an eeriness of silence over the earth just like you hear at night. But when the total eclipse was over, it was as if the earth came alive again. It was amazing to watch and hear such a phenomenon but this phenomenon created unnatural disorder.

As I walked outside, I saw an animal still asleep in the parking lot. The creature's instincts did not activate to tell it that it should not be asleep. This is what happens to us as humans when our instincts are tampered with.

When we lose our way, darkness prevails and it births confusion. Think about it. Let's say your alarm in your house went off and you have to leave work to go check on it. When you walk into your house, the first things you're probably going to turn on are your lights.

Why? Because you don't know if something is waiting for you. Yet, on the contrary when it's time to go to sleep, you cut the lights off.

The house is still your house but the circumstances by which you are in your house are different. The first situation in the dark was due to an unexpected occurrence. The second situation in the dark is more of an expectancy. The common denominator is the dark but it can mean two totally different things.

Entering the house in the dark because of a sounded alarm brings about a feeling of fear but going to sleep in the dark brings on a feeling of peace. It's all about the circumstances surrounding the darkness that create your perception of it. And so, it is the same when we begin to deal with matters of the heart. Your heart may appear one way and be totally different once it is inspected.

The heart is the most critical muscle in your body. The heart keeps blood flowing by pumping 1.5 gallons of blood per minute through your body. In fact, the heart is so important that it has its own electrical supply and can continue to beat even outside of your body. Hearts that are considered in good condition can actually last outside of the body for about four hours.

No heart is the same. Each heart has its own unique descriptors that distinguishes it from the next. Some hearts look perfectly healthy until you examine them up close. With such an intricate system within the heart, it's no surprise that heart disease is one of the greatest threats to your health.

With all these interesting facts about the heart, there is more to the heart than what the eyes can initially see. Within the heart are four hidden chambers, two atria and two ventricles. All of these chambers work together to check and balance each other, ridding itself of bad oxygen blood and replenishing itself with rich oxygen blood. We can think of bad oxygen blood as the elements that keep the heart from functioning properly and the he rich oxygen blood as the elements that sustain the heart.

The chambers also symbolize the different compartments in which we stow away our problems. We let things like pride, anger, offense, and even love feed off each other to clog our arteries. This is why we are warned to above all else guard your heart, for everything you do flows from it (Proverbs 4:23). Floating around in darkness without protection affects how we respond to conflict and everyday life. When I took a deep look at how I would react to certain situations, I found that I reacted based on what I was taught and what I saw. In some cases, it was good and in other cases, not so good. Those not so good cases were what I needed to further investigate and understand so that I could be better. Take a step back and really examine the people in your life. Their stories, both the good and the bad can give you a clue about your present.

Maybe, you're not like me and it wasn't the death of a loved one that made you plunge into a dark space but what if it was your wife or husband that caused infidelity? What if it was your family or a friend that hurt you? Or maybe you haven't forgiven yourself for that secret you didn't want anyone to find out. It is not too late to be the person you always wanted to be. I have always heard the phrase that forgiveness is not for the person who created the offense. Forgiveness is for the person that was offended and it is so true. Without it, you cage yourself into this place of distrust and your quality of life is limited.

I know you may not understand any of your pain right now but I assure you that there is a reason for all of it. Your pain is the push you needed towards your destiny. Yes, I know the residue of the pain still stings but any dark situation can turn into light through exposure to the Son. He makes all things new and brings light into utter darkness.

For those who may not believe in God or are struggling to believe right now, let me put it another way.

The earth rotates on its axis about once every 24 hours. While this is happening, half of the earth is in darkness and the other half is filled with light, causing night and day. So, night and day changes based on rotation around the sun. In other words, on the other side of the dark, you can find light.

To further illustrate my point, I remember a particular incident with a dog in my neighborhood. I was getting ready to walk to the mailbox and as soon as I opened the door, a huge pit bull came running towards me. Thank God for quick reflexes!

I slammed the door so fast I knocked the wreath off the door. The mail could wait.

I let some time pass by, thinking that the dog would be gone and I could go to the mail box. Lo and behold, as I opened the door again, the dog was watching me from one of the other neighbor's yards. It didn't move so I didn't either. I'm not usually scared of dogs but something about this dog seemed off. It was growling and I could see slobber dripping from its mouth. In my eyes, this wasn't a good look so I shut the door again.

Late that afternoon, I went back to the door to see where the dog was but to my surprise I saw animal control.

I admit. I was relieved.

Then I saw something that intrigued me. As animal control tried to force the dog into the cage with a rope, it barked and growled. I could tell the dog was not having it because it took both of the workers to get the dog in the cage. Shortly after the cage was shut, the dog tried frantically to get out to no avail. It finally quit fighting and grew silent.

Traumatic life events can take away our fight. If we don't get help, we can become a prisoner of our circumstances and accept defeat. Becoming a prisoner to your circumstances squeezes out the abundant life that is waiting for you on the other side of your wall.

It's time to tear the walls down. You were created to be free, not in bondage. Other people are depending on you to get it together because you have something to offer them.

Change your thinking and you change your perspective. If you change your perspective, you'll eventually change others around you. Separate the facts from the truth and you'll see how liberating freedom from your thoughts can be. Everything that is a fact about you is not a truth about you. Facts relay concrete ideas that cannot be objected. Truth is what is still being created, and based on what you believe to be true about you.

I can't begin to tell you how many times I had to separate fact from truth. Here are the facts. There will always be someone who doesn't like you simply because you are you. That has nothing to do with you. It has everything to do with how they feel about themselves. When you change what you think, then you can also change what you feel. You don't have to stay in the same shape. Believing and doing the same things and expecting to get a different outcome is insanity. Try something new.

To get different results, you have to try a different approach. Get beyond the walls of your offenses and fears to live freely. Acknowledge the trap and then deal with it. Freedom has been calling your name for a long time but your trap has gotten in the way. It's okay. Your way of escape has arrived. See the light.

THE ESCAPE

Destiny requires your eyes to look up for direction and your feet to blaze unfamiliar trails.

#beyondthewalls

4

SEE THE LIGHT

Challenges make you discover things about yourself that you never really knew. – Cicely Tyson

Watch out! Watch out! Bam!

A devastating blow knocked me on my back. Wait. I'm in a fight? Again? I didn't see it coming and I couldn't get up. Maybe I should just lay here. The referee started the count...One! The darkness had surrounded me and I was slowly slipping away.

Two! I was beat up badly. As I lay there, I wondered what would happen next. I couldn't come back from this.

Three! The negative words and actions of people, the expectations to live up to standards played over and over in my mind. "You're not good enough. You can't do it. You'll never reach your full potential! I've got you right where I want you. Full of doubt, full of fear!" Pow! "You're ugly". Pow! "He's not going to love you. You will continue the same familiar cycle. Who do you think you are trying to be high class?"

There was nothing left to do except close my eyes. I was tired. I didn't want to do life any more. I surely didn't want to be in another fight. Right before I slipped completely away, a voice came to me saying "Rosalind what are you doing? Get up! Get up NOW!"

The count was up to 7. I could hear people cheering me on. I heard prayers. Slowly I started stirring until I was on my feet. I fell against the ropes but I felt something or someone--a supernatural presence holding me up. The cheers and prayers were ringing in my head.

I had a renewed mind to fight but this time I was not alone.

With all the energy I had left, I swung. Right! Left! Upper Cut! POW! I gave him a blow to the head. I felt an inner power within me stirring more!!! I couldn't give up now! I was on a roll. For the first time, I was winning.

Each punch to him landed hard. I heard the crowd gasp, and then BOOM!

He hit me with sickness. My knees grew weak but I kept my hands up!

I thought about every lie that the enemy ever told me.

Not this time! I won't continue being a victim. I refuse to hide behind another wall.

I'm not giving up. I'm moving forward. As I was being held up, my balance steadied. I swung hard with all of my might and there was a loud rumble. I could barely see with my eyes but I knew he was down.

Someone in the ring with me was shouting. Eight! Nine! Ten! The bell was sounded to end the fight.

I was no longer trapped.

The scene described was a true scene in which I had the leading role. I literally was in the fight of my life. To some, it seemed I had everything. I had a nice house, a wonderful husband, and a decent job. It seemed I had everything that a girl could want but there was so much pain and hurt. I just couldn't release it on my own. My personal saving grace--two close friends who knew how to pray (one of them happened to be a counselor). That was an ugly, dark day that changed my life forever. It was all because I was tired of managing appearances.

Be the strong friend. Encourage others. Be a good wife. Be a listening ear. Shoulder this. Hide that. Give your attention over there. Show empathy. Don't cry yet. When you're pulled in so many directions, it is hard to know who you are. There is no way to be all things to all people at one time.

Keeping up appearances has become a way

of life for many. We live in a time where at one click, you can change your appearance. On pictures, we have filters. On phones, we have recording apps that allow you to change your voice. Everywhere you look, someone is always covering up something to mask a flaw or enhance a feature.

You see it happening on the news, on social media, at church, and even in the privacy of our homes. This is all because we don't want our imperfections on display. But, who does? The truth of the matter is we all have something to hide. We all struggle with insecurities. We all have heart issues.

To effectively deal with your problems, you have to take it one step or layer at a time. Peel that first layer back and ask yourself, who am I?

I don't mean what others define you as but who do you see when you look in the mirror? My best friend that I call my sister asked me this question one day. As a very busy wife and mother, it was extremely hard for me to really define who I was to myself. The first words I used to describe myself were actually these very words "wife and mother," but she told me something that baffled me. She said, "those are your roles but not who you are." I literally held the phone in silence. It dawned on me at that moment that I had lost myself. I had placed my identity on other people.

The light bulb in my mind turned on. Before I got married and we had our son, I felt as if I was on top of the world and could conquer anything. I was growing more in my faith and knew what I wanted out of life but somewhere along my path, the hush spirit came rushing in and quieted my purpose.

Now let's be clear. I am very grateful for both my husband and my son. They are my absolute greatest blessings but I came to discover there was a big part of my life missing--my identity. I've watched countless other women sink into this same demise. Freely giving but not being replenished.

I discovered in that moment that no matter

what roles you perform, your identity should never be defined through another person. Your identity is specific to you. No two people have the same DNA, not even identical twins. Identical twins have different finger prints just like everybody else. Every person on this planet has been given a unique gift that was embedded in us long before we entered the earthly realm. Jeremiah 1:5 says "Before I formed you in the womb I knew you, before you were born I set you apart; I appointed you as a prophet to the nations." You're not an imitation. You have something important enough to offer the world.

Discovery

So I want to ask you. Who are you? What makes you do the things that you do? To answer these questions, you have to take a deeper look into your heart. Discover the hidden emotional turmoil in the chambers of your heart that you so carefully stashed away over the years. Believe it or not, events of the past can leave lingering psychological effects that can spill over into our future, causing us to feel down and insecure.

One thing about being hurt, you never forget how it made you feel---whether it was abuse, the death of a loved one, or abandonment. No matter how you try to cover it up, it hurts. But you can overcome it.

The things you give residence to in your heart will shape how your relationships function in the future. What are you holding on to that's molded your identity?

Not sure? Think of it this way. The process to board a plane is you print off your flight itinerary and boarding pass, get your bags checked, go through security and then you board the plane when it's time. Before you board the plane, you have to make a decision about the luggage you will carry with you on the plane. In your case, you have two bags. Even though both pieces of luggage are the same size, you send the heavier piece to the baggage attendants to put it in a compartment under the plane.

Comparatively, this is how we alter our

true identities. What weighs the most is what gets the most attention. You never worry about the carry-on luggage because you keep it with you at all times. The luggage you sent to baggage claim, you're constantly worrying about if it's been torn open, if it will arrive to its destination, or even if there are items missing.

What weight have you chosen to carry? Your dreams and aspirations are still there. They are hidden in plain sight, making you feel miserable and frustrated about every other aspect in your life.

What often frustrates us the most is not what we are incapable of doing but what we know we can do. My dad once asked me," Rosalind are you more afraid of failing or succeeding"? I knew my answer and he did too.

Speaking from my personal experience, I never knew what it was like to be free until I allowed myself to finally be me.

Give yourself permission to be yourself. It's

okay! No amount of validation from anyone can make you be the person that you were destined to be. It all comes from within. You just have to trust the opening in the darkness and leap for it. Leave the doubts and the fears and reimagine a life on purpose. How effective you are in this life depends on how well you identified with your true self. The person God created you to be.

Now that you've discovered the opening in the wall, it's time to get up my friend. You've been down far too long.

5

GET UP AND FIGHT

You may have to fight a battle more than once to win it. – Margaret Thatcher

I am a petite young woman but I seriously struggle with exercising and eating right. Please believe me when I tell you that just because you're small does not mean that you are in great health. I mean one day I'd eat a salad and work out and the next day, I'm binge eating gummy worms, cake, chips. You name it. Then I would try to justify what I was eating like I was right.

But one day, it caught up with me when I least expected it. It started out as just a minor throat irritation, a little soreness. Nothing my allergy medicine couldn't clear up, right?

No. The irritation continued to worsen until it became painful for me to swallow. I couldn't eat or drink anything without pain. So, I went to see a doctor. The doctor prescribed meds. I took them. I started feeling better. After I was done with my prescription, the pain came back. Worse!

I knew something wasn't right. I went to another doctor and then they sent me to a specialist. By this time, my nerves got the best of me and I began to worry.

What will they find? Is there something there? Do I have a growth? What if it's not treatable?

All of these questions were sounding in my mind before I'd even seen the specialist. After careful examination, I was told it was being caused because I had a sinus infection.

Whew! A sigh of relief.

If you could have seen the smile on my face, you would have thought she'd just given me a thousand dollars. But the smile quickly faded.

She saw something else. I had irritation consistent with acid reflux. I wasn't shocked but I did not know that acid reflux could do that much damage. A previous physician had diagnosed me with it years ago but like many of us do, we ignore signals that our bodies are giving us. Again, I thought she was through telling me stuff. I was ready to get out of there.

Then she delivered the big blow. "If you don't take care of this now, you could lose your voice or become permanently hoarse."

Let me tell you. If you do any type of public speaking, singing, or even communication for your job, this is not what you want to hear.

I can't lie. I was scared, but it woke up something within me. I needed to make some major adjustments to my diet pronto!

I did and I got great results. No growth in my throat and no permanent hoarseness. Now, it's important to mention that I still have my moments of not eating properly. I am still learning but I took the initiative to not lay down and accept the diagnosis.

See, people can speak whatever over you but it's what you accept and respond to. You don't have to accept where you are. How your life turns out isn't anyone else's responsibility. It's yours. We all are accountable for our own actions. And I wholeheartedly believe that whatever your actions, you will reap one of two things either benefits or excuses.

We reap benefits by holding ourselves accountable. We reap excuses for where we are in life by constantly placing the blame on others and not handling situations as they occur. Each of us has the power to take ownership of how we react. And if we are honest with ourselves, often we'll find that we had a role to play too. Now, I'm not saying that you should reduce any offense that happened to you down to an excuse but I'm asking you, what are you going to do now? It happened. Now what? What is your next course of action? You cannot change the past but you can change your perspective. Learn to own the mess and turn it into a message. Accountability isn't an option. It is a requirement. No more partaking in the blame game. If you need to talk with someone to sort through the damage done to you mentally, go see a therapist or someone who is qualified to advise you about coping mechanisms to deal with the pain. Please understand that it is difficult to mature in a damaged state of mind. No matter how you go about picking up the pieces of your past or present, one thing remains. You have to decide to get up from where you are. The alarm is sounding.

It's time to get up.

Fight

I don't know if anyone has ever told you this or not but you're about to read something that may send shock waves through your brain. Are you ready? Here it goes. You were not meant to get up in the morning, go to work, come home, and repeat the same process. When you were designed, you were not designed to just take up space. If that were the case, you'd just be an object. A thing that can be touched or seen.

Whether you realize it, you are on an assignment. The assignment does not stop because you age. Of course, you should try to do as much as you can during your youthful days but the more you mature, the more wisdom you receive. At that point, you shift from fighting to gain to fighting to give. As a youth, you are fighting to gain wisdom and experience and as a mature individual, you fight to give the wisdom that you learned as a youth.

Isn't that something?

Throughout your entire life, you will be in a battle over something. The difference is that your perspective of the battle shifts in another direction.

On this journey to a better you, you're going to find yourself in opposition with three categories of people. Friends. Family. Frenemies. Notice I did not include "enemy" as a category. At any stage of your life, you could be in a battle with all three and I can tell you from personal experience. It will take a lot out of you and leave you feeling hopeless and faithless but the taste of victory has never been for the faint at heart. Even the small battles, scars and bruises remind you that a fight took place.

I remember as a child watching a movie called Rocky. The movie was about an Italian man named Rocky Balboa from Philadelphia who tried relentlessly to be respected in the professional world of boxing. By day, Rocky worked as a collector for a loan shark. By night, he was a boxer. It seemed that the more Rocky tried to be normal with his day job, the more uncomfortable he became. He was trying to fit where he wasn't destined to be.

Have you ever been there? You try to do the right thing and it is still not enough. Before Rocky could obtain any success in the boxing world, he had to submit to a rigorous test of his will. He had to train for the fight but he also had to know who he was fighting.

In the movie Rocky, the Italian Stallion reached a strenuous point in his life. He needed a big fight to get him notoriety but he didn't trust his potential.

A man by the name of Apollo Creed was the heavyweight boxing world champion. He was extremely confident in his ability and often gloated about it. As a promotional stunt, Creed offered a local contender from Philadelphia the chance to face him. After much deliberation and reluctance, Rocky agreed to do the fight at the urging of Mickey Goldmill a former fighter.

Mickey left nothing to be desired when it came to training Rocky. From chasing chickens to early morning running and sparring sessions, Mickey had placed Rocky in position to win. Rocky was not only physically conditioned but he was mentally prepared.

Much like Rocky, many of us don't trust our potential. Some of us are not so lucky to have someone in our corner that will motivate and push us like Rocky did. But even if you don't, here is what you know. You know your opponent and you know what your opponent is capable of. The only thing you're missing is your confidence in yourself.

Your "wall" was never about what was done to you. It's about what is on the other side of that wall. That healing. That breakthrough. That financial blessing. That self-worth. Everything that you could ever want is trapped on the other side of the wall. You have to want the wall down bad enough to get to it. If you let doubt and fear run your life, it will ruin your life. The bell in the ring didn't sound for you to get up and then lay back down at the first punch. It sounded so you can get up and stay up until the end of the match no matter how bloody it gets. A fighter never quits and a quitter never fights. Opt to be a fighter.

Don't you know that the more committed you are to becoming a "better you", the more negative reaction you will receive from others?

You're going to have to fight through some

messy situations and people. Some of your own friends and family will become jealous, hateful and unlawful in their quest to destroy you but that's a barrier that you have to break.

People who don't even know you are going to speak negatively of you because they are people. It took me a while to understand that. I thought that as long as I kept to myself and didn't bother anybody then nobody would bother me.

Boy was I wrong!

I had people spreading lies and commenting on things about me or my family that they knew nothing about. As a matter of fact, some of them I later learned were frenemies. They smiled in my face. Shook my hand and out of nowhere took a knife to my back.

In all of it, I realized that people are entitled to their opinion and you have to respect that. You can either live up to who they say you are or you can control the narrative and change their perception of you by the way you handle them. Your reactions can either help you or harm you so stay alert. Your opponent is waiting for the opportunity to push you against the ropes.

As the date approached for Rocky and Creed to fight, Rocky doubted himself tremendously. He even discredited himself with the love of his life Adrian by telling her he didn't think he was going to win. But during the match, something happened.

In boxing, timing is everything! Rocky's punches started landing. He was finally getting his timing right. Once his timing was right, the impact of the punch connected harder. The more you watch the clock, the less visible the hands of the clock become. When you're focused on the wrong thing, your timing can get thrown off. That is why it's so important to only fight when the time is right, meaning give it all you got at the appropriate time. If you take your eyes off the opponent, you'll miss your mark every time. Rocky's battle was against himself. He thought he had everything to lose when in fact, he had everything to gain.

Once he dropped the weight of the opinions of others, he was able to get in the fight.

You may not be in a battle against yourself. Your fight may be on your job, with your friends or loved ones, or maybe it's someone from your past. Don't let your escape be in vain.

When you decided to get up, you decided that you would no longer be captive to your walls. The limitations that you once placed on yourself have been removed. You can get past the sly remarks that people give. You can get past what your parents did. You can get past what you allowed to happen. You are not your past. You are on your way to who you always wanted to be. No more chains shackling you. No more darkness covering your light. The fight has come to you. How long will you last in the fight? Only you can decide.

FREEDOM

Rise, shine, and be a source of light.

6

GO FOR IT

Don't let the moment pass you by.

It has been a joy watching our son Landon grow and learn. It's so amazing to see his excitement at discovering new places and things. Sometimes he's so excited that he just can't contain himself and goes full speed ahead. We often end up running behind him chasing him or we stand somewhere close watching him in awe.

We recently went to a theme park with him and he was so overwhelmed by all of the attractions and games that he tired himself out from the all the excitement. What caught my attention even more though was not my son but a little girl that was smaller than Landon. She was with who I assume to be her parents. In that moment, I stopped and watched her. She looked up at her daddy with a big smile and started walking in her fast pace to get to whatever she was focused on. As she was headed towards it, she no longer looked at her daddy for approval. She just went after it.

This struck me for a moment because I thought to myself. How many times do we seek others' approval for something we want? This child saw nothing in her way. She only saw her goal. The crazy part about the whole situation is that I can't for the life of me tell you what she was looking at. I was captivated with her passion. She didn't show any fear. She didn't look to see who was with her. She didn't waver in where she was trying to go. Her mission was to reach her goal and nothing distracted her.

What if we had the boldness of a child discovering new things and places? Better yet, what if we applied this same attitude towards our purpose? How different do you think your life would be?

I have learned that there are times when we must exercise caution but there are also times when we must go for it. At some point, you should realize that the impossible can become possible if you focus on the end and not the beginning. You don't win a race by delaying your start. You win a race with the end in mind.

Don't let fear and doubt change your mind about your goals. I almost didn't write this book. I delayed the start of writing this book so many times because I thought about others' opinions. Then I had to realize the reason that I was writing it. To share what I've learned to help someone else. In trying to help someone else, it has allowed parts of me to completely heal.

Taking a leap of faith encourages the next person to do the same thing. See faith is going for it when you don't really know what you're seeing. Whatever goal you're trying to reach must manifest in your mind before it manifests in front of you. Going for it requires patience and stamina. It could take days, months, or years before you see what you're looking for.

Working within higher education I've seen an increase in adults returning to school (non-traditional students) because they were laid off from a job or needed a career change. The most prevalent character trait that I have witnessed from some non-traditional students is that they are intimidated easily. They look at their peers who most of the time are 10-15 years younger and immediately think their age is a stumbling block instead of an advantage.

These students are eager to start but become fearful of the complexity of the subject during the process. But, the students that continue and graduate are some of the most studious and well-prepared alumni.

Why?

They realized that to get what they've never had before they had to do things that they've never done before. They had to go for it.

What you have locked and tucked away inside of you is a treasure. It's incredible, ridiculous, and beautiful but nonetheless it's yours to discover. The only way you can do this is if you unlock what's hidden, cultivate it, and give it away. What is the treasure I'm referring to? Your gift to the world. You have always had something to offer. You just needed to know it.

Write the Vision

I've often heard the phrase, he without a plan plans to fail but I also believe that a person without a vision is blind to potential. To get the provision, there must be a vision.

Everything that you worked hard for up until this point was not just a typical climb up the mountain. You had to go through the valleys and hit some unexpected low places. You're still here. You made it! The whole point of this was to get you to see the other side of the mountainous wall. Once you have a glimpse of freedom, you can't go back to the old you. Trying to go back to the old you is like trying to fit a size 9 foot into a size 7 shoe. It just will not work.

Now that you've made discoveries about yourself and you know who you really are, there are no limits. The only limitation you can place on yourself is letting your failures get the best of you. I think you are too smart for that to happen. One thing about failure, it brings out the best in people or the worst in people. See I believe that your behavior in the low places determines the altitude for which you can survive in the higher places where there is less oxygen. What does this mean?

When you ride a rollercoaster, you don't concern yourself with your breathing until you reached the height of the coaster and it's time to come down. That final click sound is when most people breathe frantically out of excitement and fear. You can't stay at the highest altitude forever. This is why it is so important to pay attention to who is with you when you're on the way up. Are they handing you a shovel to throw dirt on yourself and complaining with you or are they extending you a hand to lift you up?

Everyone that you surround yourself with on a daily basis is not meant to have a role in your vision. Visionaries see things before they exist. You can't convince a person that can't see what they should see. Expand your thinking and look beyond your borders. Sometimes we limit ourselves to our own prejudices to keep from stepping outside our comfort zone.

I know it's hard. You finally stepped out on faith and did something that you never thought you would do and it didn't work. Failure happens. It is inevitable. But it is not the end. I never said the vision doesn't change. Maybe some characters in the vision had to move because they never fit the vision. Maybe the setting of the vision hasn't been created and you were trying to create something in a place it was never supposed to happen. You just keep writing the vision until all the components of the right vision fall into place.

7

DISTRACTIONS

Obstacles come and go. They are simply micro moments compared to the greater purpose.

I was fresh out of high school and thought I had fallen in love. Well, that feeling of love ended abruptly after finding out that the person I was in love with was heavily involved with others. I remember that day so clearly because I went for a long drive.

I felt like a fool. I trusted the potential without the evidence. As an aside to all of my single people who are waiting to be in a relationship, let the work that they have done speak for them. That was a lesson well learned.

But in taking my long drive, I ended up in

Columbia, South Carolina. I drove all the way to downtown until I couldn't drive anymore. When I looked where I was, I saw a sign that told me where I was. I was on the campus of the University of South Carolina.

I had no idea what it would take to get there. I just knew that I had to get there. I fell in love with the school without even setting foot on the campus. I know you're thinking here she goes again with trusting potential but this time it worked out. (I met my husband there!)

After circling around USC, I decided to do a little research about the school. It seemed I found the answer to all my problems. Go off to college. I can be far away from people I know and I can start over. I decided that USC would be my new home away from home.

I applied to the school and I received a letter that I was accepted. Great news, right? It was until I read further. My acceptance letter welcomed me to the university but they didn't have anywhere for me to stay. My options were to stay at a hotel and be put on a waiting list for on campus housing or delay my acceptance and attend a USC regional campus.

I was not thrilled at all! As a first-generation college student, I did not have the funds to attend USC without an adequate source of financial aid. This was turning out to be an epic failure but quitting was not an option.

With my future at USC disappearing in front of me, I made the choice to delay my acceptance. The plan was to go for a semester and then transfer to USC. That didn't happen. I liked what the regional campus was offering and I decided to continue my education there to get an associate's degree. I stayed there for two years.

In those two years, I learned more about my financial aid options and positioned myself to be more marketable for a job. I could have easily been tempted to go into the workforce full-fledged but if I did, I would have lost the opportunity to gain more experience and knowledge. I constantly had to realign myself as I made tough choices for my future. Some were good and some were bad. But I finally made it to the University of South Carolina (USC). If I had let myself be distracted by the delays, I would have missed my ultimate goal of graduating from college.

Delays are not distractions. Delays are necessary for preparation and protection. A delay is not a denial but a denial can be a delay. How can this be?

Think of it like this. When tax season approaches, the IRS sometimes provides the public with a notice that the refund process will be delayed a few weeks. In the notice, they never said the refunds wouldn't be processed. On the contrary, if the IRS processes your tax information and you don't qualify for a refund, then this would be a denial. The denial can become a delay if the conditions of the denial are no longer met. For example, the tax preparer asks you if would like to itemize deductions and you do. After review, the denial turns into a processed refund.

I mentioned delay as a distraction because there is always a negative connotation attached to this word. We never perceive it as divine protection or preparation for what is to come. Yet, we always want its benefits.

Distractions come but they can produce within you a skill that can't be taught, adaptability. Adaptability is the ability to manage or adjust to your surroundings. When you become adaptable, you learn that different settings call for different responses.

If I would have gone to USC straight out of high school, I probably would have come back home. The delay, for me was a blessing in disguise because I wasn't ready to handle that kind of responsibility. When I finally did go, I had learned the value of working hard in school, I understood and respected the wisdom from my elders, and I appreciated the experience that I received.

I was on the right track. At least, I thought I was. I found out quickly that it's easy to steer a little to the left or right when you're not balanced. As my mom would say, life can really throw you some curve balls and knock you all out of whack.

During my first year at USC, I was working two or three jobs and going to school full time. I bounced back and forth crashing at my brother's house on some weekends because I had a job in Cayce, a job in Irmo, and a job in Charlotte working at Carowinds. Talk about a bad idea to have all of these jobs and go to school! On an extremely hot day, I ended up having a heatstroke at Carowinds. That was the only job I ever left the same day and didn't come back. On top of all of this, I tried to have a little fun here and there. My study habits didn't increase or decrease. I was just doing what I would always do with all my previous classes. Take good notes and look over them a few days before the test. I figured that was enough and it's worked all of these years.

There was this one particular class that this strategy did not work well. The class was Finance 363. For me to remember the exact name of the class after ten years, you know it had to be rough! I would go to class and listen and come out of the class just as dumb as before I went. I don't think I have to tell you that things didn't end well for me with this class. I still remember the professor and for the sake of privacy, I won't mention his name. When I got my grade of a "D", that professor was the last person I wanted to see. Even though the grade is considered passing, the program that I was enrolled in, you had to at least required you to at least achieve a "C" average or above in each of your business courses.

I wasn't the only person who had challenges with this class. There were many students who complained. To me, he went too fast and there was a major communication problem.

When I got my grade, I was devastated. This was epic fail number two. One more mess up like this one for this class and I was in danger of being removed from the program completely.

I cried my eyes out! I mean I went into full blown sorrow for a few days. It was as if someone close to me had died. I knew I only had one more shot. If I couldn't get past this class, I could kiss my future goodbye. My sorrow then turned into hopelessness which then turned into regret. I should have studied more. I should have asked for help. I should have changed classes when I realized I couldn't understand my professor but I didn't. It was all because of my pride. I was overly confident in an area I had no expertise in.

I'm not the only person that this has happened to where you think you know what you're doing only to find out the hard way that you don't. Pride will lead you down a path to a point of no return if you let it, all because you refuse to acknowledge what you lack in wisdom and education. Everybody needs help at some point in their lives to propel them to the next level. See, I needed a tutor but who did you need? Who have you refused to ask for help because of your pride?

Thankfully, I had another chance. I took the

class again the next semester. I asked questions and participated in study groups. I could not let that setback distract me from my overall objective and you shouldn't either.

Distractions are meant to come from out of nowhere to disrupt your life. They test your ability to adapt. They test your pride and they test your patience. No matter what you are facing, as long as you remain grounded and lowly, you'll be fine. For a while, I kept a sticky note on my desk that said "stay low". This was my reminder that in all that I do, I should never forget who I am doing it for. One thing I have found is that if you stay low, you're less of a target.

Simply put, the more you boast on yourself, the more difficulty you will have because someone will always try to discredit you. I certainly do not want any distractions having target practice with my mind. I am graced to be able to wake up every day, not by chance but by the breath of fresh air that is breathed into me every morning by the Master. I can't afford to use my time fighting with illusions that the distractions create.

8

SOUND THE TRUMPET

Turn your mess into a message.

When the Queen of England arrives to extravagant events, she is often greeted with the sound of trumpets to announce her arrival. The coordination of the Queen entering is so seamless that it appears to happen simultaneously. At the sound of the trumpet, people know that she is coming and they stand in honor and salute her as she enters.

Trumpets have always been the instrument of choice to announce an arrival or to claim a victory. They can even be traced back to biblical history with the walls of Jericho.

Joshua, a tried and true warrior led the

Israelites to a place called Jericho to possess land that had been promised to them through a covenant God had made with their descendent Abraham. As part of Joshua's mission, he was to lead his soldiers and priests around the walls of Jericho seven times for seven days but remaining quiet until the seventh day. When the seventh day approached and they completed their assignment as God had commanded, the priests blew the trumpets and the people shouted. The wall of Jericho collapsed and the Israelites possessed the land. Isn't that a great story?

What if I said to you that this is not just a story but it is symbolic of what can happen for you too?

The Israelites were in bondage for over 400 years to the Egyptians. They finally escaped the wall of Pharaoh's heart and then wandered in the wilderness for 40 years. While in the wilderness, they had to learn and discover their new identity. With the new identity, the Israelites changed their mentality from enslaved to free. Once they understood the power of their freedom, they were able to go possess the land. The sounding of the trumpet signaled new territory for the Israelites.

Like the Israelite soldiers, you've marched around the wall in silence. The day has now come for you to see the walls in your life come down. I'm sounding the trumpet to announce your arrival. The opportunity of freedom has arrived.

The Gift of Discretion

My mom always told me that everybody who smiles in your face isn't for you. I never fully understood what this meant until I had a couple of situations in which I shared my vision with the wrong people. These same people that I trusted to be my friends ended up stabbing me in the back. As you release yourself from your own mental prison, I strongly encourage you to be aware of your surroundings. Protect your heart but also protect your vision for your future. I'm reminded of Joseph in the Bible when he dreamed of his future but then he told his brothers. His brothers got angry and secretly planned his demise. Even though Joseph got the last laugh, because he divulged too much information at the wrong time, he had to go through a process to regain his freedom. Sharing without discretion can be quite expensive.

Freedom is Calling

Everyone's idea of freedom is different yet the common factor is everybody's freedom comes with a price. At some point, we must be willing to let fear and doubt subside and let our faith rise. The only way you can walk into your destiny is if you first make a step. Put your faith in action and make the first step.

In my new found freedom, I learned that I had to take the time to smell the roses and celebrate the journey. I remember once telling someone that I didn't have the time to smell the roses. I found out quickly that life does not wait for you either. It goes on with or without your appreciation.

Honor your small beginnings. Despise not

your small beginnings because those small beginnings are the stepping stones for your future. In all things, make sure that you give thanks because you never know how your stepping stones will shift. Life moves at the speed of relationships. Those relationships are often built upon the stones.

Every journey that we take in this life is intentional because all things work together for our good. You had to go through everything you have been through to grow to what you were being stretched into. So did I.

When you have a moment, think about how far you have come. Things that used to bother you to no avail aren't as bothersome anymore. It is all because you developed the skills to handle difficult people and situations through your test and trials. You've finally learned how to walk above the noise.

Take everything you have learned about yourself and be free. Forgive yourself. Keep the rearview mirror in its proper position. Come out of depression. Choose to be a fighter and not a victim. Work to get out of debt, so you can buy that house or car you always wanted. Start a new job or even open a business. It's not too late to do any of it. Believing that it is too late can deter you before you even start. Don't let the dormant seasons fool you.

A dormant season is a season in which there is little to no activity. During the dormant season, you see frustration begin to rear its ugly head. When this happens, sow good seeds. In other words, keep working. The seeds that you scatter will one day bring forth fruit. You'll then understand why you needed a temporary pause in action.

I have come to a turning point in my life where I don't aim to be successful, I just want to be blessed. I am literally living the best days of my life right now. I have found that the best way to live is to find your happiness by doing what you are called to do. Happiness for me is not about things. It is helping others see their own potential. I love to see people create the unthinkable and break barriers and glass ceilings. It gives me great joy to witness someone doing well and walking in their purpose. That's what I want for you. You are why I wrote this book. I just wanted to share a few things that I have learned on my journey.

I am definitely not an expert at life but I am a firm believer that when you get knowledge and understanding, you should digest it, apply it, and then share it with the next person. We never perfect any part of the process. We just keep adding what we know in hopes of laying a foundation for the next person.

Now, it is your turn. The trumpet has sounded for you. The world is waiting for what you have to offer. Stand up and be of good courage. Your freedom is calling.

NOTE FROM THE AUTHOR

Thank you for reading this book and following a piece of my journey. I hope through my story a fire was ignited in you, a fire that continues to challenge you to be your best self each and every day. After all, you deserve it. My last request of you is to pass the knowledge and understanding that you received to someone else. Help someone else go beyond the walls.

As my final assignment for this book, please accept and receive the following prayer from me over your life:

I pray that you be renewed, restored, and set free. I speak peace where there is confusion and joy where there is sorrow.

I declare that your mind will be at ease and

your heart will be content. I decree courage and I denounce fear.

I stand boldly with you to proclaim that you will be blessed and that you will reap the harvest that you are gathering.

May the well of Living Water freely abide within you. In Jesus' name. Amen.

DAILY AFFIRMATIONS

1. I am not what I see but I am what I will be.

2. God did not give me a spirit of fear but of power and of love and a sound mind. (2 Timothy 1:7 NKJV)

3. I can do all things through Christ who strengthens me. (Philippians 4:13 NKJV)

4. I am an overcomer and not a victim.

REFLECTIONS

1. What ways do you feel trapped?

2. Identify a character flaw that you wish you could change. Then, think about why you wish you could change it.

3. It's often said that the thing you do naturally with very little effort is your gift. What is that one thing that you can do naturally?

4. How will you go beyond the walls to live a better life?

ACKNOWLEDGEMENTS

Throughout my life, I have been blessed to learn and glean from some of the greatest people. The wisdom and knowledge that has been shared with me is unfathomable and I am forever grateful. From the places that I've had the privilege to speak to the wonderful conversations from complete strangers, I don't take any opportunity or experience for granted.

When I decided to embark on the journey of writing this book, I had no idea how I was going to do it but I knew that I needed to brand myself so that the message would resonate. I reached out to Aaron Smalls of Aaron Smalls Photography and he just took my vision to another level. Yolanda English put her make up brush to work and brought me to life. Felicia Nicole of Hair by Felicia sculpted my hair to perfection. These are the people responsible for the cover and back matter art. Thank you.

Last but certainly not least, thank you to the Bkreative Media Solutions team for your marketing expertise and advice. All of you are so awesome and thank for your hard work in helping me be presentable.

RESOURCES

Starting a Business

Start and grow your business with the Small Business Administration at www.sba.gov.

Digital Branding
BKreative Media Solutions
www.bkreative.net

Primeview Consulting
www.primeviewconsulting.com

Looking for a New Home

Bradley Wilson
Keller Williams University City Charlotte, NC
www.bradleywilson.kwrealty.com
803-767-9760

Trauma Assistance

The National Center for Victims of Crime
VictimConnect
www.victimsofcrime.org
1-855-484-2846

Need a New Look

<u>Master Hair Care Stylist</u>
Hair by Felicia Nicole
www.FeliciaNicoleHair.com
803-235-8462

<u>Make Up Artist</u>
Yolanda IamArt English
www.facebook.com/IamArt.English
803-479-8424

Finish the New Look

Aaron D Smalls Photography
www.aarondsmalls.com

J's Photography
www.facebook.com/jaronphotography35

ABOUT THE AUTHOR

Rosalind S. Elliott is an ordinary woman given an extraordinary task. Rosalind's career in education and passion for helping others has led her to not only write this book but be an advocate for spiritual, educational and personal development. Rosalind S. Elliott lives in Columbia with her husband and child. Visit www.iamrosalindelliott.com.